On Earth as it is in Heaven

A Classic Bible Reading Guide
COMPILED BY STEPHEN L. HILL

Treasure House
An imprint of
Destiny Image
P. O. Box 310
Shippensburg, PA 17257
"For where your treasure is
there will your heart be also."
Matthew 6:21

ISBN 1-56043-797-9

LAYOUT/EDITING:
JEANINE POST
LAWRENCE ART

COVER DESIGN:
SINDI PAFFORD

SCRIPTURE QUOTATIONS:
NEW AMERICAN STANDARD VERSION
by The Lockman Foundation
Copyright 1973

*I HAVE REASONABLY ASSUMED THAT THE
AUTHORS' QUOTATIONS HEREIN WERE
PUBLIC DOMAIN.*

For Worldwide Distribution
Printed in the U.S.A.

Peace

HERE is coming a day when ...
"the wolf will dwell with the lamb,
the leopard will lie down with the kid;
the calf, the young lion and the year-
ling will feed together, and a little
child shall lead them ... At this time the earth
shall be full of the knowledge of the Lord, as
the waters cover the sea." (Isaiah 11:6,9)
How glorious it will be when this prophecy is
fulfilled and the peace of God once again
reigns upon the earth. Until then, only by
spending time with Jesus are we able to
partake of the eternal peace this beautiful
revelation portrays.

During a time of intense ministry,
Jesus said to his disciples, "come away by
yourselves to a lonely place and rest awhile".
(Mark 6:31) The Christian who learns to
spend quality time alone with our Lord will be
as a well watered tree, with his roots sinking
deep into the soil of God's heart. We nurture
our relationship with Him through prayer
and reading His Word. To the latter I dedicate
this small publication.

For over 150 years, the following Bible
reading guide has been used of God to keep
many Christians faithfully reading God's
Word. It was first published by **Robert
Murray McCheyne**, a young Scottish pastor
in the mid 1800's, over concern for his flock.

His desire was for the believers of his church to be reading the Word together, systematically, over the period of one year. In this way, he was assured that his membership was growing together. He also encouraged this guide to be used during family devotions, which allowed not only individual growth, but brought great blessings and strength to the family unit. This format takes the reader twice through the New Testament and Psalms and once through the Old Testament during the period of one year. Along with my personal Bible studies, this guide has served as a valuable tool to keep me consistently reading His Word over the years.

I encourage you to find a private place, dedicate it to God, and spend time faithfully every day with the Lord. As the Lord speaks, neatly mark in your Bible, underlining key verses and filling the margins with what God is saying to you. Allow the precious Holy Spirit time to teach you in all things.

Also included in this yearly guide are thoughts from many of our spiritual ancestors. These dedicated men and women have finished the race, fought the fight, and have left us a legacy to follow. These quotes, gleaned from my personal library, have been to me as *"apples of gold in pictures of silver."* May they serve as *"a word in season"* as you continue this pilgrimage with our Lord Jesus. I leave you with this word of encouragement from **Thomas a Kempis**:

"Lose not your confidence of making
progress toward the things of the Spirit;
you still have time,
the hour is not yet past."

Together in the Harvest,

Stephen L. Hill

On Earth as it is in Heaven

A Classic Bible Reading Guide

COMPILED BY STEPHEN L. HILL

JANUARY 1

READINGS

Genesis 1
Matthew 1
Ezra 1
Acts 1

"Remember you are not a tree, that can stand alone; you are only a branch, and it is only while you abide in Him, as a branch, that you will flourish."

**Robert M. McCheyne
(1813-1843)**

JANUARY 2

READINGS

Genesis 2
Matthew 2
Ezra 2
Acts 2

"At times we try to pump water out of a well that is dry. We pump with all our might and little water comes out. God wants our soul to be like an artesian well that can never fail of water."

**Dwight L. Moody
(1837-1899)**

JANUARY 3

READINGS

Genesis 3
Matthew 3
Ezra 3
Acts 3

"Satan gives Adam an apple (fruit), and takes away Paradise. Therefore in all temptations let us consider not what he offers, but what we shall lose."

**Richard Sibbes
(1577-1635)**

JANUARY 4

READINGS

Genesis 4
Matthew 4
Ezra 4
Acts 4

"Sins are like circles in the water when a stone is thrown into it: one produces another. When anger was in Cain's heart, murder was not far off."

**Philip Henry
(1631-1696)**

JANUARY 5

READINGS

Genesis 5
Matthew 5
Ezra 5
Acts 5

"It is no use to talk of leaning on God while at the same time we are, in one way or another, looking to some poor mortal to help us."

**Charles H. Mackintosh
(1820-1896)**

JANUARY 6

READINGS

Genesis 6
Matthew 6
Ezra 6
Acts 6

"I care not where I live, or what hardships I go through, so that I can but gain souls to Christ. All my desire is the conversion of sinners, and all my hope is in God."

**David Brainerd
(1717-1747)**

JANUARY 7

Genesis 7
Matthew 7
Ezra 7
Acts 7

"Give what Thou wilt, and how much Thou wilt, and when Thou wilt. Send me where Thou wilt and deal with me in all things, just as Thou wilt."

Thomas a Kempis
(1380-1471)

JANUARY 8

READINGS

Genesis 8
Matthew 8
Ezra 8
Acts 8

"Give me one hundred men who fear nothing but sin, and desire nothing but God, and I will shake the world."

John Wesley
(1703-1791)

JANUARY 9

READINGS

Genesis 9-10
Matthew 9
Ezra 9
Acts 9

"He that closes his eyes at night without prayer, lies down before his bed is made."

William Gurnall
(1617-1679)

3

JANUARY 10

READINGS

Genesis 11
Matthew 10
Ezra 10
Acts 10

"For there is nothing that makes us love a man so much as praying for him; and when you can once do this sincerely for any man, you have fitted your soul for the performance of everything that is kind and civil towards him."

**William Law
(1686-1761)**

JANUARY 11

READINGS

Genesis 12
Matthew 11
Nehemiah 1
Acts 11

"It is good to be humbled. I am never better than when I am brought to lie at the foot of the cross. It is a certain sign God intends that soul a greater crown."

**George Whitefield
(1714-1770)**

JANUARY 12

READINGS

Genesis 13
Matthew 12
Nehemiah 2
Acts 12

"As much as God desires the salvation of men, He will not prostitute heaven, and set the gates of it wide open to those who only fly to it in extremity but never sought it in good earnest, nor indeed do now care for it, or desire it for any other reason, but to excuse them from going to hell."

**Richard Baxter
(1615-1691)**

4

JANUARY 13

Genesis 14
Matthew 13
Nehemiah 3
Acts 13

"It is not great talents God blesses so much as great likeness to Jesus. A holy minister is an awful weapon in the hand of God."

Robert M. McCheyne
(1813-1843)

JANUARY 14

Genesis 15
Matthew 14
Nehemiah 4
Acts 14

"We may feel God's hand as a Father upon us when He **strikes** us as well as when He **strokes** us."

Abraham Wright
(1611-1690)

JANUARY 15

Genesis 16
Matthew 15
Nehemiah 5
Acts 15

"How shall I depend on Him for raising my body from the dust and saving my soul at last, if I distrust Him for a crust of bread towards my preservation?"

Joseph Hall
(1574-1656)

JANUARY 16

Genesis 17
Matthew 16
Nehemiah 6
Acts 16

"Prayer is as natural an expression of faith as breathing is of life; and to say a man lives a life of faith, and yet lives a prayerless life, is every bit as inconsistent and incredible as to say that a man lives without breathing."

**Jonathon Edwards
(1703-1758)**

JANUARY 17

Genesis 18
Matthew 17
Nehemiah 7
Acts 17

"What a difference in men who go into battle intending to conquer **if they can**, and those who go into battle intending to conquer."

**Dwight L. Moody
(1837-1899)**

JANUARY 18

Genesis 19
Matthew 18
Nehemiah 8
Acts 18

"Our failing is dreadful, our falling is shameful, and our dying is sorrowful; but in all this the sweet eye of pity and love is never lifted off us, nor the working of mercy ceaseth."

**Lady Julian of Norwich
(1342-1413)**

JANUARY 19

READINGS

Genesis 20
Matthew 19
Nehemiah 9
Acts 19

"I have nothing to seek but the glory of God; nothing to fear but His displeasure."

Francis Asbury
(1745-1816)

JANUARY 20

READINGS

Genesis 21
Matthew 20
Nehemiah 10
Acts 20

"He did what He taught, and He taught what He did. He came to serve and to give, and His whole life was marked by those two things, from the manger to the cross."

Charles H. Mackintosh
(1820-1896)

JANUARY 21

READINGS

Genesis 22
Matthew 21
Nehemiah 11
Acts 21

"Humility is nothing but the disappearance of self in the vision that God is all."

Andrew Murray
(1828-1917)

JANUARY 22

READINGS

Genesis 23
Matthew 22
Nehemiah 12
Acts 22

"Nothing, in such a world as this, can be more foolish than to renounce a friend because we have found him to be imperfect."

Susan Huntington
(1791-1823)

JANUARY 23

READINGS

Genesis 24
Matthew 23
Nehemiah 13
Acts 23

"If you want to enrich a man, do not increase his riches, but diminish or alter his desires!"

J. B. Stoney
(1815-1897)

JANUARY 24

READINGS

Genesis 25
Matthew 24
Esther 1
Acts 24

"The more able to wait long for answers to our desires and prayers, the stronger faith is."

William Gurnall
(1617-1679)

JANUARY 25

READINGS

Genesis 26
Matthew 25
Esther 2
Acts 25

"A man's greatest care should be for that place where he lives longest; therefore eternity should be his scope."

Thomas Manton
(1620-1677)

JANUARY 26

READINGS

Genesis 27
Matthew 26
Esther 3
Acts 26

"One smile from Jesus sustains my soul amid all the storms and frowns of this passing world. Pray to know Jesus better."

Robert M. McCheyne
(1813-1843)

JANUARY 27

READINGS

Genesis 28
Matthew 27
Esther 4
Acts 27

"There are no crownwearers in Heaven that were not crossbearers here below."

Charles H. Spurgeon
(1834-1892)

JANUARY 28

READINGS

Genesis 29
Matthew 28
Esther 5
Acts 28

"Believers find rich mines of silver and gold in solitary places; they fetch up precious jewels out of secret holes, out of the bottom of the ocean, where there are no inhabitants."

George Swinnock
(1627-1673)

JANUARY 29

READINGS

Genesis 30
Mark 1
Esther 6
Romans 1

"The godly man, when he dies, enters into peace; but, while he lives, peace must enter into him."

Thomas Watson
(1620-1686)

JANUARY 30

READINGS

Genesis 31
Mark 2
Esther 7
Romans 2

"A long time out of Christ's glorious presence is two deaths and two hells for me. We must meet. I am not able to do without Him."

Samuel Rutherford
(1600-1661)

JANUARY 31

"Nearness to God is the foundation of a creature's happiness."

Isaac Watts
(1674-1748)

THE RAISING OF JAIRUS' DAUGHTER

FEBRUARY 1

"It is not so much praying for direction that one needs as getting near the Lord; and the nearer you are to Him, the clearer will everything appear."

J. B. Stoney
(1815-1897)

11

FEBRUARY 2

Genesis 34
Mark 5
Job 1
Romans 5

"Nothing is more essential to an acceptable approach to God in the duties of His worship in general, and particularly in receiving the seals of His covenant, than a thorough and universal separation from all known sin."

John Witherspoon
(1722-1749)

FEBRUARY 3

Genesis 35-36
Mark 6
Job 2
Romans 6

"According to the **weight** of the burden that grieves us is the **cry** to God that comes from us."

Joseph Caryl
(1602-1673)

FEBRUARY 4

Genesis 37
Mark 7
Job 3
Romans 7

"The fame of being a godly man is as great a snare as the fame of being learned or eloquent. It is possible to attend with scrupulous anxiety even to secret habits of devotion, in order to get a name for holiness."

Robert M. McCheyne
(1813-1843)

FEBRUARY 5

READINGS

Genesis 38
Mark 8
Job 4
Romans 8

"If God be your partner, make your plans large."

Dwight L. Moody
(1837-1899)

FEBRUARY 6

READINGS

Genesis 39
Mark 9
Job 5
Romans 9

"Until the fear of the Lord gets its true place in the heart, there can be nothing right, nothing wise, nothing holy. How can there be, if indeed that fear is the beginning of wisdom?"

Charles H. Mackintosh
(1820-1896)

FEBRUARY 7

READINGS

Genesis 40
Mark 10
Job 6
Romans 10

"Oh that the Lord would saturate us through and through with an undying zeal for the souls of men."

Charles H. Spurgeon
(1834-1892)

FEBRUARY 8

READINGS

Genesis 41
Mark 11
Job 7
Romans 11

"The more ready and prepared the Christian is to suffer for God, or from God, the more God is engaged to take care for him and of him."

William Gurnall
(1617-1679)

FEBRUARY 9

READINGS

Genesis 42
Mark 12
Job 8
Romans 12

"There is nothing like the oil of mercy, so potent a solvent for an iron heart."

Samuel Lee
(1625-1691)

FEBRUARY 10

READINGS

Genesis 43
Mark 13
Job 9
Romans 13

"Sin, carried far enough, becomes its own punishment."

Samuel Annesley
(1620-1696)

FEBRUARY 11

Genesis 44
Mark 14
Job 10
Romans 14

"Real satisfaction can only come to the heart of your Lord when you seem to be 'wasting' yourself on the Lord, giving too much and getting nothing back for yourself."

Watchman Nee
(1903-1972)

FEBRUARY 12

READINGS

Genesis 45
Mark 15
Job 11
Romans 15

"Humility is a strange flower; it grows best in the winter weather, and under storms of affliction."

Samuel Rutherford
(1600-1661)

FEBRUARY 13

READINGS

Genesis 46
Mark 16
Job 12
Romans 16

"It is utterly vain and delusive to profess to be living by faith and looking to the Lord, while in reality our hearts are looking to some creature resource."

Charles H. Mackintosh
(1820-1896)

FEBRUARY 14

READINGS

Genesis 47
Luke 1:1-38
Job 13
1 Corinthians 1

"Let the seas roar, the earth be shaken, and all things go to ruin and confusion; yet, the soul that adheres to God will remain safe and quiet, and shall not be moved for ever."

**Robert Leighton
(1613-1684)**

FEBRUARY 15

READINGS

Genesis 48
Luke 1:39-80
Job 14
1 Corinthians 2

"The most important part of my prayers are the fifteen minutes after I say 'Amen'."

**George Mueller
(1805-1898)**

FEBRUARY 16

READINGS

Genesis 49
Luke 2
Job 15
1 Corinthians 3

"Lord, send me much sore and trying calamities as shall awake me from earthly slumbers. It must always be best to be alive to Thee, whatever be the quickening instrument."

**Robert M. McCheyne
(1813-1843)**

FEBRUARY 17

READINGS

**Genesis 50
Luke 3
Job 16-17
1 Corinthians 4**

"The fire is kindled in the country *(England)*, and all the devils in hell shall not be able to quench it."

**George Whitefield
(1714-1770)**

FEBRUARY 18

READINGS

**Exodus 1
Luke 4
Job 18
1 Corinthians 5**

"The greatness of a man's power is the measure of his surrender."

**William Booth
(1829-1912)**

FEBRUARY 19

READINGS

**Exodus 2
Luke 5
Job 19
1 Corinthians 6**

"When our minds are filled with God, suffering will become full of sweetness, of unction, and of quiet joy."

**Nicolas Herman
(Brother Lawrence)
(1611-1691)**

FEBRUARY 20

READINGS

Exodus 3
Luke 6
Job 20
1 Corinthians 7

"Where God loves, He afflicts in love, and wherever God afflicts in love, there He will first and last teach such souls such lessons as shall do them good to all eternity."

**Thomas Brooks
(1608-1680)**

FEBRUARY 21

READINGS

Exodus 4
Luke 7
Job 21
1 Corinthians 8

"I feel it is far better to begin the day with God, to see His face first, to get my soul near Him before it is near another."

**Robert M. McCheyne
(1813-1843)**

FEBRUARY 22

READINGS

Exodus 5
Luke 8
Job 22
1 Corinthians 9

"He that takes no care to set forth God's portion of time in the morning, doth not only rob God of His due, but is a thief to himself all the day after, by losing the blessing which a faithful prayer might bring from heaven on his undertaking."

**William Gurnall
(1617-1679)**

FEBRUARY 23

Exodus 6
Luke 9
Job 23
1 Corinthians 10

"Groanings which cannot be uttered are often prayers which cannot be refused."

Charles H. Spurgeon
(1834-1892)

FEBRUARY 24

Exodus 7
Luke 10
Job 24
1 Corinthians 11

"It does not say, make your light shine. If it is really a light it will shine in spite of you - only don't hide it under a bushel. Let it shine. Confess Christ everywhere."

Dwight L. Moody
(1837-1899)

FEBRUARY 25

Exodus 8
Luke 11
Job 25-26
1 Corinthians 12

"A man shall as soon force fruit out of a branch broken off from the tree and withered as work righteousness without believing in, and uniting with, Christ."

Thomas Boston
(1676-1732)

FEBRUARY 26

READINGS

Exodus 9
Luke 12
Job 27
1 Corinthians 13

"Surely profound words do not make a man holy and just; but a virtuous life makes him dear to God."

**Thomas a Kempis
(1380-1471)**

FEBRUARY 27

READINGS

Exodus 10
Luke 13
Job 28
1 Corinthians 14

"When God created man, to find his blessedness in entire dependence upon Him, and in receiving all life and goodness each moment from Him, **humility** was the one condition of his continuing in that blessed state."

**William Law
(1686-1761)**

FEBRUARY 28

READINGS

Exodus 11-12:21
Luke 14
Job 29
1 Corinthians 15

"I never feel comfortable, but when I find my soul going forth after God."

**David Brainerd
(1717-1747)**

MARCH 1

Exodus 12:22-51
Luke 15
Job 30
1 Corinthians 16

"At the cross, the battle was fought and the victory won; and now the liberal hand of sovereign grace is scattering far and wide the spoils of victory."

Charles H. Mackintosh
(1820-1896)

MARCH 2

READINGS

Exodus 13
Luke 16
Job 31
2 Corinthians 1

"We walk in this world as a man in a field of snow; all the way appears smooth, yet we cannot be sure of any step."

Thomas Adams
(1614-1670)

MARCH 3

READINGS

Exodus 14
Luke 17
Job 32
2 Corinthians 2

"He that is merciful to sin is cruel to his own soul."

Ralph Venning
(1620-1673)

MARCH 4

READINGS

Exodus 15
Luke 18
Job 33
2 Corinthians 3

"The moral excellency and beauty of divine things; the glory and loveliness of the divine nature, law and Gospel - spiritually discerned, are the **grand** preservative against every error and every abuse in religion."

Thomas Scott
(1747-1821)

MARCH 5

READINGS

Exodus 16
Luke 19
Job 34
2 Corinthians 4

"The work of a Christian lies not in the depth of speculation, but in the height of practice."

Thomas Manton
(1620-1677)

MARCH 6

READINGS

Exodus 17
Luke 20
Job 35
2 Corinthians 5

"There is a Godly sorrow which leads a man to life, and this sorrow is wrought in a man by the Spirit of God, and in the heart of the godly, that he mourns for sin because it has displeased God, who is so dear and so sweet a Father to him."

John Welch
(1576-1622)

MARCH 7

READINGS

Exodus 18
Luke 21
Job 36
2 Corinthians 6

"No one loses God, but he that is willing to part with Him."

**William Gurnall
(1617-1679)**

MARCH 8

READINGS

Exodus 19
Luke 22
Job 37
2 Corinthians 7

"Praise and thanksgiving are the most delectable business of heaven; and God grant they may be our greatest delight, our most frequent employment upon earth!"

**Isaac Barrow
(1630-1705)**

MARCH 9

READINGS

Exodus 20
Luke 23
Job 38
2 Corinthians 8

"For a frequent intercession with God, earnestly beseeching Him to forgive the sins of all mankind, to lessen them with His providence, enlighten them with His Spirit, and bring them to everlasting happiness, is the divinest exercise that the heart of man can be engaged in."

**William Law
(1686-1761)**

MARCH 10

READINGS

Exodus 21
Luke 24
Job 39
2 Corinthians 9

"To pursue everlasting happiness as the end, in the way of holiness as the mean, this is 'wisdom,' this is common sense, and there can be none without this."

**Samuel Davies
(1724-1761)**

MARCH 11

READINGS

Exodus 22
John 1
Job 40
2 Corinthians 10

"The tongue never made itself to speak, and yet talks against Him that did; saying, that which is made, **is**, and that which made it, **is not**."

**Jeremy Taylor
(1613-1667)**

MARCH 12

READINGS

Exodus 23
John 2
Job 41
2 Corinthians 11

"I ought to spend the best hours of the day in communion with God. It is my noblest and most fruitful employment, and is not to be thrust into any corner."

**Robert M. McCheyne
(1813-1843)**

MARCH 13

READINGS

Exodus 24
John 3
Job 42
2 Corinthians 12

"Behold what a God have we! View Him well and take notice how glorious a God He is."

**John Howe
(1630-1705)**

MARCH 14

READINGS

Exodus 25
John 4
Proverbs 1
2 Corinthians 13

"Go for souls - and go for the worst."

**Gen. William Booth
(1829-1912)**

MARCH 15

READINGS

Exodus 26
John 5
Proverbs 2
Galatians 1

"I never got away from Jesus and Him crucified in my preaching. I found that once people were gripped by the great meaning of Christ's sacrifice on our behalf, I did not have to give them many instructions about changing their behavior."

**David Brainerd
(1717-1747)**

MARCH 16

READINGS

Exodus 27
John 6
Proverbs 3
Galatians 2

"As the firmament is bespangled with stars, so are the sacred pages with promises and divine engagements."

Stephen Charnock
(1628-1680)

MARCH 17

READINGS

Exodus 28
John 7
Proverbs 4
Galatians 3

"Choose rather to want less, than to have more."

Thomas a Kempis
(1380-1471)

MARCH 18

READINGS

Exodus 29
John 8
Proverbs 5
Galatians 4

"Take up every cross; never turn aside to avoid one; you will always find two in the place of it; go into every open door, and cry unto Him continually to be endued with power from on high."

John Summerfield
(1770-1825)

MARCH 19

Exodus 30
John 9
Proverbs 6
Galatians 5

"It is of little use talking of faith if the heart be a stranger to its power. Mere profession is perfectly worthless."

Charles H. Mackintosh
(1820-1896)

MARCH 20

Exodus 31
John 10
Proverbs 7
Galatians 6

"The road to heaven is soaked with the tears and blood of the saints."

William S. Plumer
(1802-1880)

MARCH 21

Exodus 32
John 11
Proverbs 8
Ephesians 1

"Let the devil choose his way; God is a match for him at every weapon. The devil and his whole council are but fools to God; nay, their wisdom foolishness."

William Gurnall
(1617-1679)

MARCH 22

Exodus 33
John 12
Proverbs 9
Ephesians 2

"I feel there are two things it is impossible to desire with sufficient ardour - personal holiness and the honour of Christ in the salvation of souls."

Robert M. McCheyne
(1813-1843)

MARCH 23

READINGS

Exodus 34
John 13
Proverbs 10
Ephesians 3

"God's ways being the safest, cleanest, rightest, shortest, and lightsomest ways, we must be careful to walk in them."

Thomas Taylor
(1576-1632)

MARCH 24

READINGS

Exodus 35
John 14
Proverbs 11
Ephesians 4

"We cannot seek God till we have found Him."

George Swinnock
(1627-1673)

MARCH 25

READINGS

Exodus 36
John 15
Proverbs 12
Ephesians 5

"A sin of infirmity may admit apology, a sin of ignorance may find out excuse, but a sin of defiance can find no defense."

Sir Richard Baker
(1568-1645)

MARCH 26

READINGS

Exodus 37
John 16
Proverbs 13
Ephesians 6

"He holdeth our soul in life, that it may not drop away of itself; for being continually in our hands, it is apt to slip through our fingers."

Matthew Henry
(1662-1714)

MARCH 27

READINGS

Exodus 38
John 17
Proverbs 14
Philippians 1

"The thorn is one of the most cursed and angry and crabbed weeds that the earth yields, and yet out of it springs the rose, one of the sweetest flowers, and most delightful to the eye."

Samuel Rutherford
(1600-1661)

MARCH 28

READINGS

Exodus 39
John 18
Proverbs 15
Philippians 2

"There is nothing more deceitful than your estimate of your own strength."

Robert M. McCheyne
(1813-1843)

MARCH 29

READINGS

Exodus 40
John 19
Proverbs 16
Philippians 3

"Satan watcheth for those vessels that sail without a convoy."

George Swinnock
(1627-1673)

MARCH 30

READINGS

Leviticus 1
John 20
Proverbs 17
Philippians 4

"A man who prays much in private will make short prayers in public."

Dwight L. Moody
(1837-1899)

MARCH 31

READINGS
Leviticus 2-3
John 21
Proverbs 18
Colossians 1

"We are a supernatural people, born again by a supernatural birth; we wage a supernatural fight and are taught by a supernatural teacher, led by a supernatural captain to assured victory."

**James Hudson Taylor
(1832-1905)**

CHRIST BLESSING LITTLE CHILDREN

APRIL 1

READINGS
Leviticus 4
Psalms 1-2
Proverbs 19
Colossians 2

"Faith tells the soul what Christ hath done for it, and so comforts it; hope revives the soul with the news of what Christ will do; both draw at one tap - Christ and His promise."

**William Gurnall
(1617-1679)**

APRIL 2

READINGS

Leviticus 5
Psalms 3-4
Proverbs 20
Colossians 3

"Meditation is a spiritual index; the index shows what is in the book, so meditation shows what is in the heart."

Thomas Watson
(1620-1686)

APRIL 3

READINGS

Leviticus 6
Psalms 5-6
Proverbs 21
Colossians 4

"I'll spend my life to my latest moments in dens and caves of the earth, if the Kingdom of Christ may be advanced."

David Brainerd
(1717-1747)

APRIL 4

READINGS

Leviticus 7
Psalms 7-8
Proverbs 22
1 Thessalonians 1

"If you have never walked in the path of obedience before, do so now, and you will then know experimentally the sweetness of the joy which results from it."

George Mueller
(1805-1898)

APRIL 5

READINGS

Leviticus 8
Psalm 9
Proverbs 23
1 Thessalonians 2

"The only way to keep a broken vessel full is to keep it always under the tap."

**Dwight L. Moody
(1837-1899)**

APRIL 6

READINGS

Leviticus 9
Psalm 10
Proverbs 24
1 Thessalonians 3

"We ought to propose to ourselves, to become, in this life, the most perfect worshippers of God we can possibly be, as we hope to be through all eternity."

**Nicolas Herman
(Brother Lawrence)
(1611-1691)**

APRIL 7

READINGS

Leviticus 10
Psalms 11-12
Proverbs 25
1 Thessalonians 4

"If their houses were on fire, thou wouldst run and help them; and wilt thou not help them when their souls are almost at the fire of hell?" *(concerning witnessing to your neighbors)*

**Richard Baxter
(1615-1691)**

33

APRIL 8

READINGS

Leviticus 11-12
Psalms 13-14
Proverbs 26
1 Thessalonians 5

"A calm hour with God is worth a whole lifetime with man."

Robert M. McCheyne
(1813-1843)

APRIL 9

READINGS

Leviticus 13
Psalms 15-16
Proverbs 27
2 Thessalonians 1

"Bear and forbear, and silent be,
tell to no man thy misery;
Yield not in trouble to dismay,
God can deliver any day."

Martin Luther
(1483-1546)

APRIL 10

READINGS

Leviticus 14
Psalm 17
Proverbs 28
2 Thessalonians 2

"True godliness evermore wears upon her head the garland of perseverance."

William Couper
(1566-1619)

APRIL 11

READINGS

Leviticus 15
Psalm 18
Proverbs 29
2 Thessalonians 3

"He who provides for this life, but takes no care for eternity, is wise for a moment, but a fool forever."

John Tillotson
(1630-1694)

APRIL 12

READINGS

Leviticus 16
Psalm 19
Proverbs 30
1 Timothy 1

"By the **fear of the Lord** men depart from evil; by the **fear of man** they run themselves into evil."

John Flavel
(1627-1691)

APRIL 13

READINGS

Leviticus 17
Psalms 20-21
Proverbs 31
1 Timothy 2

"Morality may keep you out of jail, but it takes the blood of Jesus Christ to keep you out of hell."

Charles H. Spurgeon
(1834-1892)

APRIL 14

READINGS

Leviticus 18
Psalm 22
Ecclesiastes 1
1 Timothy 3

"There is no such thing in Scripture as the forgiveness of sin. God has condemned sin, not forgiven it - an immensely important distinction."

**Charles H. Mackintosh
(1820-1896)**

APRIL 15

READINGS

Leviticus 19
Psalms 23-24
Ecclesiastes 2
1 Timothy 4

"The Bible, prayer, the House of God -- these are the golden pipes through which the golden oil is poured."

**Robert M. McCheyne
(1813-1843)**

APRIL 16

READINGS

Leviticus 20
Psalm 25
Ecclesiastes 3
1 Timothy 5

"All temporal things are troublesome: for if we have good things, it is a trouble to forego them; and when we see they must be parted from, either we wish they had not been so good, or that we never had enjoyed them."

**Joseph Hall
(1574-1656)**

APRIL 17

READINGS

Leviticus 21
Psalms 26-27
Ecclesiastes 4
1 Timothy 6

"Whoever be our people here, God's people or the devil's, death will gather our souls to them."

**Thomas Boston
(1676-1732)**

APRIL 18

READINGS

Leviticus 22
Psalms 28-29
Ecclesiastes 5
2 Timothy 1

"God expects to hear from you, before you can expect to hear from Him. If thou restrainest prayer, it is no wonder the mercy promised is retained."

**William Gurnall
(1617-1679)**

APRIL 19

READINGS

Leviticus 23
Psalm 30
Ecclesiastes 6
2 Timothy 2

"I look upon all the world as my parish; that in whatever part of it I am, I judge it meet, right and my bounden duty to declare unto all that are willing to hear, the glad tidings of salvation."

**John Wesley
(1703-1791)**

APRIL 20

READINGS

Leviticus 24
Psalm 31
Ecclesiastes 7
2 Timothy 3

"Our great problem is the problem of trafficking in unlived truth. We try to communicate what we've never experienced in our own life."

**Dwight L. Moody
(1837-1899)**

APRIL 21

READINGS

Leviticus 25
Psalm 32
Ecclesiastes 8
2 Timothy 4

"A child of five, if properly instructed, can as truly believe and be regenerated as an adult."

**Charles H. Spurgeon
(1834-1892)**

APRIL 22

READINGS

Leviticus 26
Psalm 33
Ecclesiastes 9
Titus 1

"When we have nothing, we can trust the Lord for everything."

**J. B. Stoney
(1815-1897)**

APRIL 23

READINGS

Leviticus 27
Psalm 34
Ecclesiastes 10
Titus 2

"There is only one way to keep you from sin; that is, persevering resistance to temptation, and prayer."

Susan Huntington
(1791-1823)

APRIL 24

READINGS

Numbers 1
Psalm 35
Ecclesiastes 11
Titus 3

"He that is greater than all the world is looking with the intensest interest upon all your steps."

Robert M. McCheyne
(1813-1843)

APRIL 25

READINGS

Numbers 2
Psalm 36
Ecclesiastes 12
Philemon 1

"The service of Christ is a very solemn and a very holy thing; and all who take part therein must be self-judged, self-distrusting, and self-emptied; and not only so, but they must lean, with unshaken confidence, upon the living God."

Charles H. Mackintosh
(1820-1896)

APRIL 26

READINGS

Numbers 3
Psalm 37
Song of Solomon 1
Hebrews 1

"Can anything in this world be more foolish than to think that all this rare fabric of heaven and earth can come by chance, when all the skill of art is not able to make an oyster?"

**Jeremy Taylor
(1613-1667)**

APRIL 27

READINGS

Numbers 4
Psalm 38
Song of Solomon 2
Hebrews 2

"One **Almighty** is more than **all mighties**."

**William Gurnall
(1617-1679)**

APRIL 28

READINGS

Numbers 5
Psalm 39
Song of Solomon 3
Hebrews 3

"The man of pride has a thousand wants, which only his own pride has created; and these render him as full of trouble as if God had created him with a thousand appetites, without creating anything that was proper to satisfy them."

**William Law
(1686-1761)**

"On the following words I staked everything, and they never failed, 'Lo, I am with you always, even unto the end of the world'."

**David Livingstone
(1813-1873)**

"Be not, therefore, too confident in thine own opinion; but be willing to hear the judgment of others."

**Thomas a Kempis
(1380-1471)**

THE PRODIGAL SON

MAY 1

**Numbers 8
Psalm 44
Song of Solomon 6
Hebrews 6**

"And thou knowest, O Lord, that in these matters I am not accustomed to being denied." *(concerning intercession for the lost)*

**Charles G. Finney
(1792-1875)**

MAY 2

**Numbers 9
Psalm 45
Song of Solomon 7
Hebrews 7**

"He who has enabled us to stick to Him will surely stick to us."

**Charles H. Spurgeon
(1834-1892)**

MAY 3

**Numbers 10
Psalms 46-47
Song of Solomon 8
Hebrews 8**

"The world may frown - Satan may rage - but go on! Live for God. May I die in the field of battle."

**James B. Taylor
(1801-1829)**

MAY 4

Numbers 11
Psalm 48
Isaiah 1
Hebrews 9

"You are all guilt; He is a fountain to wash you. You are all naked; He has a wedding garment to cover you. You are dead; He is the life. You are all wounds and bruises; He is the Balm of Gilead."

Robert M. McCheyne
(1813-1843)

MAY 5

READINGS

Numbers 12-13
Psalm 49
Isaiah 2
Hebrews 10

"I wish to bear testimony to the fact that we can do **no good** without a broken and contrite heart."

Ira D. Sankey
(1840-1908)

MAY 6

READINGS

Numbers 14
Psalm 50
Isaiah 3-4
Hebrews 11

"As to gold and silver, I count it dung and dross; I trample it under my feet; I esteem it just as the mire of the streets. I desire it not and I seek it not; I only fear lest any of it should cleave to me, and I should not be able to shake it off before my spirit returns to God."

John Wesley
(1703-1791)

MAY 7

READINGS

Numbers 15
Psalm 51
Isaiah 5
Hebrews 12

"A coward heart will not do for the day of battle; a doubting spirit will not stand in conflict."

Charles H. Mackintosh
(1820-1896)

MAY 8

READINGS

Numbers 16
Psalms 52-54
Isaiah 6
Hebrews 13

"It's not under the **sharpest**, but the **longest** trials that we are most in danger of fainting."

Andrew Fuller
(1754-1815)

MAY 9

READINGS

Numbers 17-18
Psalm 55
Isaiah 7
James 1

"All those things that now please us shall pass from us, or we from them; but those things that concern the other life are permanent as the numbers of eternity."

Jeremy Taylor
(1613-1667)

MAY 10

READINGS

Numbers 19
Psalms 56-57
Isaiah 8-9:7
James 2

"That which makes anybody esteem us, is their knowledge or apprehension of some little good, and their ignorance of a great deal of evil that may be in us; were they thoroughly acquainted with us, they would quickly change their opinion."

**Henry Scougal
(1650-1678)**

MAY 11

READINGS

Numbers 20
Psalms 58-59
Isaiah 9:8-10:4
James 3

"Contention is the devil's forge, in which, if he can but give a Christian a heat or two, he will not doubt but to soften him for his hammer of temptation."

**William Gurnall
(1617-1679)**

MAY 12

READINGS

Numbers 21
Psalms 60-61
Isaiah 10:5-34
James 4

"When Adam was away, Eve was made a prey."
(concerning Godly marriage)

**Henry Smith
(1560-1591)**

MAY 13

READINGS

Numbers 22
Psalms 62-63
Isaiah 11-12
James 5

"I don't very often spend more than half an hour without praying."

Smith Wigglesworth
(1859-1947)

MAY 14

READINGS

Numbers 23
Psalms 64-65
Isaiah 13
1 Peter 1

"When our affections are alive to other things, they are dead to God, therefore the less we let loose our hearts to these things, the more lively and cheerful in the work of obedience."

Thomas Manton
(1620-1677)

MAY 15

READINGS

Numbers 24
Psalms 66-67
Isaiah 14
1 Peter 2

"For some years it has been my abiding conviction that it is impossible to enjoy true happiness without being entirely devoted to God."

David Brainerd
(1717-1747)

MAY 16

Numbers 25
Psalm 68
Isaiah 15
1 Peter 3

"It is always a good proof that your convictions and desires are from the operation of the Spirit when you are willing to conform to God's order."

William Jay
(1769-1853)

MAY 17

READINGS

Numbers 26
Psalm 69
Isaiah 16
1 Peter 4

"There is nothing that you can possibly need but you will find it in Him."

Robert M. McCheyne
(1813-1843)

MAY 18

READINGS

Numbers 27
Psalms 70-71
Isaiah 17-18
1 Peter 5

"I have read of some barbarous nations who, when the sun shines hot upon them, shoot up their arrows against it - so do wicked men the light and heat of godliness."

Jeremiah Burroughs
(1599-1646)

47

MAY 19

READINGS

Numbers 28
Psalm 72
Isaiah 19-20
2 Peter 1

"A Christian is growing when he elevates his Master, talks less of what he himself is doing, and becomes smaller and smaller in his own esteem; until, like the morning star, he fades away before the rising sun."

**Horatius Bonar
(1808-1889)**

MAY 20

READINGS

Numbers 29
Psalm 73
Isaiah 21
2 Peter 2

"You may meet with princes in this world, but except you be born again, you cannot meet the Prince of Peace."

**Dwight L. Moody
(1837-1899)**

MAY 21

READINGS

Numbers 30
Psalm 74
Isaiah 22
2 Peter 3

"We must know before we can love. In order to know God, we must often think of Him; and when we come to love Him, we shall also think of Him often, for our heart will be with our treasure!"

**Nicolas Herman
(Brother Lawrence)
(1611-1691)**

MAY 22

READINGS

Numbers 31
Psalms 75-76
Isaiah 23
1 John 1

"God is not like men, who make large promises, but either through inability, or carelessness, or unfaithfulness, do not perform them; but will certainly be as good as His Word."

Matthew Pool
(1624-1679)

MAY 23

READINGS

Numbers 32
Psalm 77
Isaiah 24
1 John 2

"The **stops** of a good man are ordered by the Lord as well as his steps."

George Mueller
(1805-1898)

MAY 24

READINGS

Numbers 33
Psalm 78:1-37
Isaiah 25
1 John 3

"It is simply impossible to be near Christ, and not have the heart filled with the sweetest affections for all that belong to Him."

Charles H. Mackintosh
(1820-1896)

49

MAY 25

READINGS

Numbers 34
Psalm 78:38-72
Isaiah 26
1 John 4

"The greater the guilt of any sinner is, the more glorious and wonderful is the grace manifested in his pardon."

Jonathan Edwards
(1703-1758)

MAY 26

READINGS

Numbers 35
Psalm 79
Isaiah 27
1 John 5

"When we are free and in prosperity ourselves, we must not be unmindful of our brethren that are in trouble and under restraint."

Matthew Henry
(1662-1714)

MAY 27

READINGS

Numbers 36
Psalm 80
Isaiah 28
2 John 1

"Pity those ye have left behind you in **black** nature, 'without God, and without Christ, and without hope in the world.' Endeavour their salvation. Commend Christ to them by your practice and by your conversation."

Thomas Halyburton
(1674-1712)

MAY 28

READINGS

Deuteronomy 1
Psalms 81-82
Isaiah 29
3 John 1

"The best way to deal with slander is to pray about it: God will either remove it, or remove the sting from it."

**Charles H. Spurgeon
(1834-1892)**

MAY 29

READINGS

Deuteronomy 2
Psalms 83-84
Isaiah 30
Jude 1

"The Christian's great conquest over the world is all contained in the mystery of Christ upon the cross."

**William Law
(1686-1761)**

MAY 30

READINGS

Deuteronomy 3
Psalm 85
Isaiah 31
Revelation 1

"Seek much personal holiness and likeness to Christ in all the features of His blessed character. Seek to be lamb-like, without which all your efforts to do good to others will be as sounding brass or a tinkling cymbal."

**Robert M. McCheyne
(1813-1843)**

MAY 31

"He that thinks to please men goes about an endless and needless work. A wise physician seeks to cure, not please, his patient." *(on duties of ministers regarding preaching the Word)*

William Gurnall
(1617-1679)

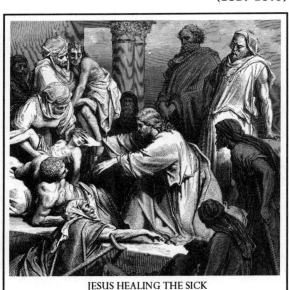

JESUS HEALING THE SICK

JUNE 1

"God alone sees the heart; the heart alone sees God."

John Donne
(1573-1631)

JUNE 2

READINGS

Deuteronomy 6
Psalm 89
Isaiah 34
Revelation 4

"If there is anything of power in my ministry today, it is because God has all the adoration of my heart, all the power of my will, and all the influence of my life."

William Booth
(1829-1912)

JUNE 3

READINGS

Deuteronomy 7
Psalm 90
Isaiah 35
Revelation 5

"A family without prayer is like a house without a roof; it has no protection."

William Jay
(1769-1853)

JUNE 4

READINGS

Deuteronomy 8
Psalm 91
Isaiah 36
Revelation 6

"The **greatness** of God rouses fear within us, but His **goodness** encourages us not to be afraid of Him. To fear and not be afraid - that is the paradox of faith."

A. W. Tozer
(1897-1963)

JUNE 5

READINGS

Deuteronomy 9
Psalms 92-93
Isaiah 37
Revelation 7

"In a world system darkened with the smoke of the pit, how we rejoice to meet saints who are fresh with the clean air of heaven."

Watchman Nee
(1903-1972)

JUNE 6

READINGS

Deuteronomy 10
Psalm 94
Isaiah 38
Revelation 8

"You need not be afraid of covetousness in spiritual things; rather 'covet earnestly' to increase your store."

Charles Bridges
(1794-1869)

JUNE 7

READINGS

Deuteronomy 11
Psalms 95-96
Isaiah 39
Revelation 9

"I have only one passion; it is He, He alone."

Nicholas L. Zinzendorf
(1700-1760)

JUNE 8

Deuteronomy 12
Psalms 97-98
Isaiah 40
Revelation 10

"Let the Holy Spirit fill every chamber of your heart; and so there will be no room for folly, or the world, or Satan, or the flesh."

**Robert M. McCheyne
(1813-1843)**

JUNE 9

Deuteronomy 13-14
Psalms 99-101
Isaiah 41
Revelation 11

"The debt we owe to the past we must endeavor to repay by handing down the Truth to the future."

**Charles H. Spurgeon
(1834-1892)**

JUNE 10

Deuteronomy 15
Psalm 102
Isaiah 42
Revelation 12

"The most successful searches have been made in the night season; the soul is then wholly shut up in the earthly house of the body, and hath no visits from strangers to disquiet its thoughts."

**George Swinnock
(1627-1673)**

JUNE 11

READINGS

Deuteronomy 16
Psalm 103
Isaiah 43
Revelation 13

"The sweet bait of religion hath drawn many to nibble at it who are offended with the hard services it calls to. It requires another spirit than the world can give or receive to follow Christ fully."

**William Gurnall
(1617-1679)**

JUNE 12

READINGS

Deuteronomy 17
Psalm 104
Isaiah 44
Revelation 14

"There is no greater hindrance to our getting into the thoughts of God than having our minds filled with our own thoughts, or the thoughts of men."

**Charles H. Mackintosh
(1820-1896)**

JUNE 13

READINGS

Deuteronomy 18
Psalm 105
Isaiah 45
Revelation 15

"Love to Christ will enable us to make sacrifices for Him without feeling it to be a hardship."

**Dwight L. Moody
(1837-1899)**

JUNE 14

READINGS

Deuteronomy 19
Psalm 106
Isaiah 46
Revelation 16

"It has always been my aim, and it is my prayer to have no plan as regards myself; well assured as I am that the place where the Saviour sees meet to place me must ever be the best place for me."

Robert M. McCheyne
(1813-1843)

JUNE 15

READINGS

Deuteronomy 20
Psalm 107
Isaiah 47
Revelation 17

"It is not poverty, but discontent that makes a man unhappy."

Matthew Henry
(1662-1714)

JUNE 16

READINGS

Deuteronomy 21
Psalms 108-109
Isaiah 48
Revelation 18

"Death to self means a total despair of self - that is, to give up all thoughts of having or doing anything that is good in any other way but that of a meek, humble, patient, total resignation of ourselves to God."

William Law
(1686-1761)

JUNE 17	**READINGS**

Deuteronomy 22
Psalms 110-111
Isaiah 49
Revelation 19

"Fatigues and hardships serve to wean me from the earth; and I trust will make heaven the sweeter."

David Brainerd
(1717-1747)

JUNE 18	**READINGS**

Deuteronomy 23
Psalms 112-113
Isaiah 50
Revelation 20

"A hungry, craving appetite after Christ and sweet satisfaction in Him are inseparable, and still the stronger is our appetite, the greater is our satisfaction."

Joseph Cary
(1602-1673)

JUNE 19	**READINGS**

Deuteronomy 24
Psalms 114-115
Isaiah 51
Revelation 21

"Do not think that thou hast made any progress unless thou esteem thyself inferior to all."

Thomas a Kempis
(1380-1471)

JUNE 20

READINGS

Deuteronomy 25
Psalm 116
Isaiah 52
Revelation 22

"Lord, open the king of England's eyes." *(Martyr-last words spoken - was tied to the stake, strangled, and consumed with fire.)*

**William Tyndale
(1484-1536)**

JUNE 21

READINGS

Deuteronomy 26
Psalms 117-118
Isaiah 53
Matthew 1

"The world is not a playground; it is a schoolroom. Life is not a holiday, but an education. And the one eternal lesson for us all is **how better we can love**."

**Henry Drummond
(1851-1897)**

JUNE 22

READINGS

Deut. 27-28:19
Psalm 119:1-24
Isaiah 54
Matthew 2

"Evil may ferment, wrath may boil, and pride may foam, but the brave heart of holy confidence trembles not."

**Charles H. Spurgeon
(1834-1892)**

JUNE 23

READINGS

Deut. 28:20-68
Psalm 119:25-48
Isaiah 55
Matthew 3

"The Scripture is the compass by which the rudder of our will is to be steered; it is the field in which Christ, the Pearl of Great Price, is hid."

Thomas Watson
(1620-1686)

JUNE 24

READINGS

Deuteronomy 29
Psalm 119:49-72
Isaiah 56
Matthew 4

"Labour without God cannot prosper; labour against God and against His Will in His Word, will surely miscarry."

Thomas Manton
(1620-1677)

JUNE 25

READINGS

Deuteronomy 30
Psalm 119:73-96
Isaiah 57
Matthew 5

"God delights to be fully counted upon and largely used. The deeper the need, and the darker the surrounding gloom, the more is He glorified by the faith that draws upon Him."

Charles H. Mackintosh
(1820-1896)

JUNE 26

READINGS

Deuteronomy 31
Psalm 119:97-120
Isaiah 58
Matthew 6

"Christians are compared to a tree in the first Psalm. Trees that flourish most and bear the sweetest fruit are those which stand most in the sun."

**William Gurnall
(1617-1679)**

JUNE 27

READINGS

Deuteronomy 32
Psalm 119:121-144
Isaiah 59
Matthew 7

"Let every new sight of your wicked heart, and every new wave of trouble drive your soul to hide in Him, the Rock of your salvation."

**Robert M. McCheyne
(1813-1843)**

JUNE 28

READINGS

Deuteronomy 33
Psalm 119:145-176
Isaiah 60
Matthew 8

"The fathers are passing away, and breaches are daily making in the ranks of the standard bearers. Oh, that God would raise up a host of pious youths ardently waiting to catch the standards before they fall from the veterans of the cross."

**John Summerfield
(1770-1825)**

READINGS

Joshua 1
Psalms 120-122
Isaiah 61
Matthew 9

"If men were as much in earnest to get their souls saved as they are to prepare them for perdition, heaven would be highly peopled, and devils would be their own companions."

**Adam Clarke
(1762-1832)**

JUNE
30

READINGS

Joshua 2
Psalms 123-125
Isaiah 62
Matthew 10

"You may look with pleasure upon the jewelled crowns of the earth, but unless you be born again you cannot see the Crown of Life."

**Dwight L. Moody
(1837-1899)**

THE MIRACLE OF THE LOAVES AND FISHES

"Go to poor sinners with tears in your eyes, that they may see you believe them to be miserable, and that you unfeignedly pity their case. Let them perceive it is the desire of your heart to do them good."

Richard Baxter
(1615-1691)

"The more able to wait long for answers to our desires and prayers, the stronger faith is."

William Gurnall
(1617-1679)

"Some flowers must be broken and bruised before they emit any fragrance. All the wounds of Christ send out sweetness; all the sorrows of Christians do the same."

Robert M. McCheyne
(1813-1843)

JULY 4

READINGS

Joshua 6:6-27
Psalms 135-136
Isaiah 66
Matthew 14

"As every good master or father of a family is a good preacher to his own family, so every good Christian is a good preacher to his own soul."

Richard Baxter
(1615-1691)

JULY 5

READINGS

Joshua 7
Psalms 137-138
Jeremiah 1
Matthew 15

"The powers of darkness are not to be feared, for the Lord, our Light, destroys them; and the damnation of hell is not to be dreaded by us, for the Lord is our salvation."

Charles H. Spurgeon
(1834-1892)

JULY 6

READINGS

Joshua 8
Psalm 139
Jeremiah 2
Matthew 16

"Age makes other things decay, but a Christian flourish. His trees bring forth fruit in old age."

Stephen Charnock
(1628-1680)

READINGS

Joshua 9
Psalms 140-141
Jeremiah 3
Matthew 17

"Read and read again ... for a little from God is better than a great deal from man; what is from man is uncertain, lost and tumbled over and over; but what is from God is as fixed as a nail in a sure place."

John Bunyan
(1628-1688)

READINGS

Joshua 10
Psalms 142-143
Jeremiah 4
Matthew 18

"It remains for the world to see what the Lord can do with a man wholly consecrated to Christ."

Henry Varley
(1835-1912)

READINGS

Joshua 11
Psalm 144
Jeremiah 5
Matthew 19

"Those were the words of the Lord, through your lips to my soul." *(Spoken in response to Henry Varley's statement listed above. It has been said that Mr. Moody based his entire ministry upon this truth.)*

Dwight L. Moody
(1837-1899)

"Secure sinners must hear the thundering of Mount Sinai before we bring them to Mount Zion. Every minister should be a Boanerges, a son of thunder, as well as Barnabas, a son of consolation."

George Whitefield
(1714-1770)

"Pilgrims forget the scanty supply at an **inn**, when they have abundance in view at the end."

Andrew Bonar
(1810-1892)

"Unless the common course of our lives be according to the common course of our prayers, our prayers are so far from being a real or sufficient degree of devotion that they become an empty lip-labour or, what is worse, a notorious hypocrisy."

William Law
(1686-1761)

JULY 13

"The heart should be a house of prayer; Christ will not endure to have it a place of merchandise. Either thou must whip these buyers and sellers out, or the Spirit will go out."

William Gurnall
(1617-1679)

JULY 14

"We have all eternity in which to enjoy our victories, but only one short life in which to win them."

David Livingstone
(1813-1873)

JULY 15

"I had one joy out of heaven next to Christ my Lord, and that was to preach Him to this faithless generation; and they have taken that from me. It was to me as the poor man's one eye, and they have put out that eye." *(Imprisoned for preaching the Gospel)*

Samuel Rutherford
(1600-1661)

JULY 16

"Affliction without the Word is a furnace for the metal, but there is no flux to aid the purifying: the Word of God supplies that need, and makes the fiery trial effectual."

**Charles H. Spurgeon
(1834-1892)**

JULY 17

"There is a wide difference between the feelings produced by dwelling upon our sins and those which flow from dwelling upon the sufferings of Christ to put those sins away."

**Charles H. Mackintosh
(1820-1896)**

JULY 18

"He was under violent pain in the garden and on the cross; ineffable was the sorrow that He felt, being forsaken of His Father, deserted by His disciples, affronted and reproached by His enemies, and under a curse for us."

**Timothy Rogers
(1660-1729)**

JULY 19

READINGS

Judges 2
Acts 6
Jeremiah 15
Mark 1

"Let the Word not only **inform** you, but **inflame** you."

**Thomas Watson
(1620-1686)**

JULY 20

READINGS

Judges 3
Acts 7
Jeremiah 16
Mark 2

"God hath given to man a short time here upon earth and yet upon this short time eternity depends. No man is a better merchant than he that lays out his time upon God."

**Jeremy Taylor
(1613-1667)**

JULY 21

READINGS

Judges 4
Acts 8
Jeremiah 17
Mark 3

"Expect great things from God; attempt great things for God."

**William Carey
(1761-1834)**

JULY 22

READINGS

Judges 5
Acts 9
Jeremiah 18
Mark 4

"You may stand on the banks of many mighty rivers, but except you be born again you never can see the river that bursts from the Throne of God and runs through His Kingdom."

**Dwight L. Moody
(1837-1899)**

JULY 23

READINGS

Judges 6
Acts 10
Jeremiah 19
Mark 5

"To be without Jesus is a grievous hell, and to be with Jesus, a sweet paradise."

**Thomas a Kempis
(1380-1471)**

JULY 24

READINGS

Judges 7
Acts 11
Jeremiah 20
Mark 6

"The Scriptures teach us the best way of living, the noblest way of suffering, and the most comfortable way of dying."

**John Flavel
(1627-1691)**

JULY 25

READINGS

Judges 8
Acts 12
Jeremiah 21
Mark 7

"I will never spend more time in any matter of mere recreation in one day, than I spend in private Christian duties!"

**Susanna Wesley
(Mother of the Wesleys)
(1669-1742)**

JULY 26

READINGS

Judges 9
Acts 13
Jeremiah 22
Mark 8

"I set myself on fire, and the people come to see me burn." *(when asked how he got the crowds)*

**John Wesley
(1703-1791)**

JULY 27

READINGS

Judges 10-11:11
Acts 14
Jeremiah 23
Mark 9

"Oh, cry for personal holiness, constant nearness to God by the Blood of the Lamb! Bask in His beams; lie back in the arms of love; be filled with the Spirit; or all success in the ministry will only be to your own everlasting confusion."

**Robert M. McCheyne
(1813-1843)**

JULY 28

READINGS

Judges 11:12-40
Acts 15
Jeremiah 24
Mark 10

"The beginning of anxiety is the end of faith. The beginning of true faith is the end of anxiety."

George Mueller
(1805-1898)

JULY 29

READINGS

Judges 12
Acts 16
Jeremiah 25
Mark 11

"A **neglected** Saviour will be a **severe** Judge."

Thomas Boston
(1676-1732)

JULY 30

READINGS

Judges 13
Acts 17
Jeremiah 26
Mark 12

"The great thing is to be growing up unto Christ. The young Christian who is growing is more interesting and more helpful to others than the most advanced one who is stationary."

J. B. Stoney
(1815-1897)

JULY 31

READINGS

**Judges 14
Acts 18
Jeremiah 27
Mark 13**

"If Christ has not the love of your heart, He does not want the labor of your hands."

**Charles H. Mackintosh
(1820-1896)**

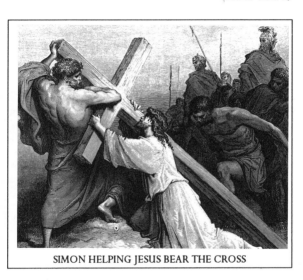

SIMON HELPING JESUS BEAR THE CROSS

AUGUST 1

READINGS

**Judges 15
Acts 19
Jeremiah 28
Mark 14**

"I feel persuaded that if I could follow the Lord more fully myself, my ministry would be used to make a deeper impression than it has yet done."

**Robert M. McCheyne
(1813-1843)**

AUGUST 2

READINGS

**Judges 16
Acts 20
Jeremiah 29
Mark 15**

"After a man is a Christian, I work him day and night. I believe that for one man killed by over-work in the cause of Christ ten thousand die from laziness."

**Dwight L. Moody
(1837-1899)**

AUGUST 3

READINGS

**Judges 17
Acts 21
Jeremiah 30-31
Mark 16**

"A man whose heart is not watered with the dew of God's grace continually may for a time make a fair show of godliness, but in the end he will fall away."

**William Couper
(1566-1619)**

AUGUST 4

READINGS

**Judges 18
Acts 22
Jeremiah 32
Psalms 1-2**

"What lust is so sweet or profitable that is worth burning in hell for? Is any lust so precious in thy eye that thou canst not leave it behind thee, rather than fall into the hands of God's justice?"

**William Gurnall
(1617-1679)**

READINGS

Judges 19
Acts 23
Jeremiah 33
Psalms 3-4

"I am more afraid of my own heart than of the Pope and all his Cardinals. I have within me the great pope, SELF."

Martin Luther
(1483-1546)

READINGS

Judges 20
Acts 24
Jeremiah 34
Psalms 5-6

"If we are obeying the Lord, the responsibility rests with Him, not with us. We must obey the Scriptures and trust God to be faithful to His pledged Word."

James Hudson Taylor
(1832-1905)

READINGS

Judges 21
Acts 25
Jeremiah 35
Psalms 7-8

"*Lo, I am with you always, even unto the end of the age.* That's the word of a perfect gentleman, and that's the end of it."

David Livingstone
(1813-1873)

AUGUST 8

READINGS

Ruth 1
Acts 26
Jeremiah 36,45
Psalm 9

"Remember God never gives light for two steps at a time. If He has given thee light for one step, then in the fear and love of His Name, take that one step, and thou assuredly will get more light."

**Charles H. Mackintosh
(1820-1896)**

AUGUST 9

READINGS

Ruth 2
Acts 27
Jeremiah 37
Psalm 10

"Before you are aware, the evil contracted through the eyes creeps in to the inmost recesses of the heart, and casts in the seeds of perdition."

**Wolfgang Musculus
(1497-1563)**

AUGUST 10

READINGS

Ruth 3-4
Acts 28
Jeremiah 38
Psalms 11-12

"Fellowship with the stem begets fertility in the branches. If a man abide in Christ he brings forth much fruit."

**Charles H. Spurgeon
(1834-1892)**

AUGUST 11

READINGS

1 Samuel 1
Romans 1
Jeremiah 39
Psalms 13-14

"Your own soul is your first and greatest care. Keep up close communion with God. Read the Bible for your own growth first, then for your people. You will not find many companions." *(to a pastor)*

Robert M. McCheyne
(1813-1843)

AUGUST 12

READINGS

1 Samuel 2
Romans 2
Jeremiah 40
Psalms 15-16

"When I have any money, I get rid of it as quickly as possible, lest it find a way into my heart."

John Wesley
(1703-1791)

AUGUST 13

READINGS

1 Samuel 3
Romans 3
Jeremiah 41
Psalm 17

"Devotion which consists in times and forms of prayer is but a very small thing, if compared to that devotion which is to appear in every other part and circumstance of our lives."

William Law
(1686-1761)

AUGUST 14

READINGS

1 Samuel 4
Romans 4
Jeremiah 42
Psalm 18

"His eye is upon every hour of my existence. His Spirit is intimately present with every thought of my heart. His inspiration gives birth to every purpose within me. His hand impresses a direction on every footstep of my goings."

Thomas Chalmers
(1780-1847)

AUGUST 15

READINGS

1 Samuel 5-6
Romans 5
Jeremiah 43
Psalm 19

"I cannot imagine how religious persons can live satisfied without the practice of the presence of God."

Nicolas Herman
(Brother Lawrence)
(1611-1691)

AUGUST 16

READINGS

1 Samuel 7-8
Romans 6
Jeremiah 44
Psalms 20-21

"I believe many backsliders are still Christians outwardly, but they have been moving away in heart. They neglect secret prayer and become very formal in public devotion."

Dwight L. Moody
(1837-1899)

AUGUST 17

1 Samuel 9
Romans 7
Jeremiah 46
Psalm 22

"The more humble a man is in himself, and the more subject unto God, the more wise and peaceful shall he be in all things."

**Thomas a Kempis
(1380-1471)**

AUGUST 18

1 Samuel 10
Romans 8
Jeremiah 47
Psalms 23-24

"I make it a rule of Christian duty never to go to a place where there is not room for my Master as well as myself."

**John Newton
(1725-1807)**

AUGUST 19

1 Samuel 11
Romans 9
Jeremiah 48
Psalm 25

"We behold at the cross the marvelous meeting of enmity and love - sin and grace. Man displayed at Calvary the very height of his enmity against God. God, blessed be His Name, displayed the height of His love. Hatred and love met."

**Charles H. Mackintosh
(1820-1896)**

AUGUST 20

READINGS

1 Samuel 12
Romans 10
Jeremiah 49
Psalms 26-27

"Holy ones, in every age, have lived near to God in secret. It is this that fits one to live a holy, self-denying, cross-bearing life before the world."

**James B. Taylor
(1801-1829)**

AUGUST 21

READINGS

1 Samuel 13
Romans 11
Jeremiah 50
Psalms 28-29

"Every dislike of evil is not sufficient; but perfect **hatred** is required of us against all sorts and degrees of sin."

**David Dickson
(1583-1662)**

AUGUST 22

READINGS

1 Samuel 14
Romans 12
Jeremiah 51
Psalm 30

"The Christian's armour decays two ways, either by violent battery when the Christian is overcome by temptation to sin, or else by neglecting to furbish and scour it with the use of those means which are as oil, to keep it clean and bright."

**William Gurnall
(1617-1679)**

AUGUST 23

READINGS

1 Samuel 15
Romans 13
Jeremiah 52
Psalm 31

"That which is rotten will sooner corrupt that which is sound, than be cured or made sound by it."

Matthew Henry
(1662-1714)

AUGUST 24

READINGS

1 Samuel 16
Romans 14
Lamentations 1
Psalm 32

"Temporal prosperity is too small a matter to be worth fretting about; let the dogs have their bones, and the swine their draff."

Charles H. Spurgeon
(1834-1892)

AUGUST 25

READINGS

1 Samuel 17
Romans 15
Lamentations 2
Psalm 33

"If the cause be removed, the effects will cease. If the spring be purified, the waters will be healed, and the barren ground become productive."

Andrew Fuller
(1754-1815)

AUGUST 26

READINGS

1 Samuel 18
Romans 16
Lamentations 3
Psalm 34

"Let me endure any thing rather than Thine absence and displeasure; and desire nothing so much as Thy presence and favor."

Benjamin Jenks
(1646-1724)

AUGUST 27

READINGS

1 Samuel 19
1 Corinthians 1
Lamentations 4
Psalm 35

"The Lord doth not only fit work for us, but fits us for our work; with His command He gives power."

Thomas Watson
(1620-1686)

AUGUST 28

READINGS

1 Samuel 20
1 Corinthians 2
Lamentations 5
Psalm 36

"Wherever we go, we see that God's mercy and truth have been there by the deep tracks they have left behind them."

Adam Clarke
(1762-1832)

AUGUST 29

READINGS

1 Samuel 21-22
1 Corinthians 3
Ezekiel 1
Psalm 37

"Prayer is, if I may so speak, the very breath of the new creature; as soon as it is created, it prays; so that where there is an habitual neglect of secret prayer, there is no faith."

Thomas Halyburton
(1674-1712)

AUGUST 30

READINGS

1 Samuel 23
1 Corinthians 4
Ezekiel 2
Psalm 38

"Past answers to prayer should encourage us to come the more boldly to the Throne of Grace."

William S. Plumer
(1802-1880)

AUGUST 31

READINGS

1 Samuel 24
1 Corinthians 5
Ezekiel 3
Psalm 39

"Many who are great in the sight of the Lord are living in cottages and hovels, and are scarcely known, unless to a few neighbors equally obscure."

William Jay
(1769-1853)

SEPTEMBER 1

READINGS

1 Samuel 25
1 Corinthians 6
Ezekiel 4
Psalms 40-41

"All questions of the **plane** should be settled on the Mount, and where there is certainty in the Mount there will be victory on the levels and in the valley."

**Samuel Chadwick
(1860-1932)**

SEPTEMBER 2

READINGS

1 Samuel 26
1 Corinthians 7
Ezekiel 5
Psalms 42-43

"There was an earthquake and a whirlwind before the small, still voice came to Elijah - we must first show people they are condemned, and then show them how they must be saved."

**George Whitefield
(1714-1770)**

SEPTEMBER 3

READINGS

1 Samuel 27
1 Corinthians 8
Ezekiel 6
Psalm 44

"The depth of devotion - without this depth our crying out of other depths will never be heard."

**Sir Richard Baker
(1568-1645)**

SEPTEMBER 4

READINGS

1 Samuel 28
1 Corinthians 9
Ezekiel 7
Psalm 45

"We may lull the soul asleep with carnal delights, but the virtue of that opium will be soon spent."

Thomas Manton
(1620-1677)

SEPTEMBER 5

READINGS

1 Samuel 29-30
1 Corinthians 10
Ezekiel 8
Psalms 46-47

"The Word is the only weapon for the hewing down and cutting off of this stubborn enemy - our lusts."

William Gurnall
(1617-1679)

SEPTEMBER 6

READINGS

1 Samuel 31
1 Corinthians 11
Ezekiel 9
Psalm 48

"The ark only had one entrance. The eagle had to come down to enter it; and the worm had to crawl up to it."

Charles H. Spurgeon
(1834-1892)

SEPTEMBER 7

READINGS

2 Samuel 1
1 Corinthians 12
Ezekiel 10
Psalm 49

"No person can be a child of God without living in secret prayer; and no community of Christians can be in a lively condition without unity in prayer."

Robert M. McCheyne
(1813-1843)

SEPTEMBER 8

READINGS

2 Samuel 2
1 Corinthians 13
Ezekiel 11
Psalm 50

"There is no happiness in having or in getting, but only in giving. Half the world is on the wrong scent in pursuit of happiness."

Henry Drummond
(1851-1897)

SEPTEMBER 9

READINGS

2 Samuel 3
1 Corinthians 14
Ezekiel 12
Psalm 51

"The Church should never become fixed, earth-bound, static. God Himself takes away His workers, but He gives others. Our work suffers, but His never does. Nothing touches Him. He is still God."

Watchman Nee
(1903-1972)

SEPTEMBER 10

READINGS

2 Samuel 4-5
1 Corinthians 15
Ezekiel 13
Psalms 52-54

"God knows how to prepare the heart for the message and the message for the heart."

Charles H. Mackintosh
(1820-1896)

SEPTEMBER 11

READINGS

2 Samuel 6
1 Corinthians 16
Ezekiel 14
Psalm 55

"A heathen philosopher once asked, 'Where is God?' The Christian answered, 'Let me first ask you, where is He not?'"

John Arrowsmith
(1602-1659)

SEPTEMBER 12

READINGS

2 Samuel 7
2 Corinthians 1
Ezekiel 15
Psalms 56-57

"That which a man spits against Heaven shall fall back on his own face." *(concerning final judgment)*

Thomas Adams
(1585-1630)

87

SEPTEMBER 13

READINGS

**2 Samuel 8-9
2 Corinthians 2
Ezekiel 16
Psalms 58-59**

"The wages that sin **bargains** with the sinner are life, pleasure, and profit; but the wages it **pays** him with are death, torment, and destruction."

**Robert South
(1633-1716)**

SEPTEMBER 14

READINGS

**2 Samuel 10
2 Corinthians 3
Ezekiel 17
Psalms 60-61**

"For years Jesus has been leading me where I never could have gone myself."

**Dwight L. Moody
(1837-1899)**

SEPTEMBER 15

READINGS

**2 Samuel 11
2 Corinthians 4
Ezekiel 18
Psalms 62-63**

"Secret tears for secret sins are an excellent sign of a holy heart, and a healing balsam for broken spirits. God well understands the language of half words interrupted with sighs, and interprets them as the streams and breathings of a broken heart."

**Samuel Lee
(1625-1691)**

SEPTEMBER 16

READINGS

2 Samuel 12
2 Corinthians 5
Ezekiel 19
Psalms 64-65

"He that puts the treasure into earthen vessels often allows the vessel to be chipped and broken that the excellency of the power may be of God and not of us."

**Robert M. McCheyne
(1813-1843)**

SEPTEMBER 17

READINGS

2 Samuel 13
2 Corinthians 6
Ezekiel 20
Psalms 66-67

"He is the best friend at all times, and the only friend at sometimes."

**Joseph Caryl
(1602-1673)**

SEPTEMBER 18

READINGS

2 Samuel 14
2 Corinthians 7
Ezekiel 21
Psalm 68

"I cared not where or how I lived, or what hardships I endured so that I could but gain souls for Christ. While I was asleep I dreamt of such things, and when I waked the first thing I thought of was winning souls to Christ."

**David Brainerd
(1717-1747)**

SEPTEMBER 19

READINGS

2 Samuel 15
2 Corinthians 8
Ezekiel 22
Psalm 69

"I will praise God whether He deals with me in a way of justice or in a way of mercy, when He hath thunder in His voice, as well as when He hath honey under His tongue."

**Stephen Charnock
(1628-1680)**

SEPTEMBER 20

READINGS

2 Samuel 16
2 Corinthians 9
Ezekiel 23
Psalms 70-71

"Nearness to Christ will draw us nearer to each other." *(concerning true Christian fellowship)*

**Andrew Murray
(1828-1917)**

SEPTEMBER 21

READINGS

2 Samuel 17
2 Corinthians 10
Ezekiel 24
Psalm 72

"Men do not drop into the right way by chance; they must choose it, and continue to choose it, or they will soon wander from it."

**Charles H. Spurgeon
(1834-1892)**

SEPTEMBER 22

READINGS

**2 Samuel 18
2 Corinthians 11
Ezekiel 25
Psalm 73**

"God makes the most perfect work of all in the dark, for He fashions man in the mother's womb."

**John Calvin
(1509-1564)**

SEPTEMBER 23

READINGS

**2 Samuel 19
2 Corinthians 12
Ezekiel 26
Psalm 74**

"A helpless infant, or a harmless lamb, surrounded by furious bulls and hungry lions, aptly represents the Saviour encompassed by His insulting and bloody persecutors."

**Thomas Scott
(1747-1821)**

SEPTEMBER 24

READINGS

**2 Samuel 20
2 Corinthians 13
Ezekiel 27
Psalms 75-76**

"No Christian is in a right condition, if he is not seeking in some way to bring souls to Christ."

**Charles H. Mackintosh
(1820-1896)**

SEPTEMBER 25

READINGS

2 Samuel 21
Galatians 1
Ezekiel 28
Psalm 77

"The sweet spices of divine works must be beaten to powder by meditation, and then laid up in the cabinet of our memories."

**Abraham Wright
(1611-1690)**

SEPTEMBER 26

READINGS

2 Samuel 22
Galatians 2
Ezekiel 29
Psalm 78:1-37

"Lose not your confidence of making progress toward the things of the Spirit; you still have time, the hour is not yet past."

**Thomas a Kempis
(1380-1471)**

SEPTEMBER 27

READINGS

2 Samuel 23
Galatians 3
Ezekiel 30
Psalm 78:38-72

"The Scriptures are a spiritual physic-garden where grows an herb for the cure of every malady."

**William Gurnall
(1617-1679)**

SEPTEMBER 28

READINGS

2 Samuel 24
Galatians 4
Ezekiel 31
Psalm 79

"Deal gently and tenderly with your unconverted friends. Remember, you were once as blind as they."

Robert M. McCheyne
(1813-1843)

SEPTEMBER 29

READINGS

1 Kings 1
Galatians 5
Ezekiel 32
Psalm 80

"A man may go to hell with baptismal water upon his face."

John Trapp
(1601-1669)

SEPTEMBER 30

READINGS

1 Kings 2
Galatians 6
Ezekiel 33
Psalms 81-82

"Full resignation to God's will, a wholehearted giving up of ourselves to the blessed perfect will of God, will bring perfect rest."

William Law
(1686-1761)

OCTOBER 1

READINGS

1 Kings 3
Ephesians 1
Ezekiel 34
Psalms 83-84

"How inexcusable shall I be if I should starve in the midst of such abundance, and perish when Thou hast sent me such great salvation!"

Symon Patrick
(1626-1707)

OCTOBER 2

READINGS

1 Kings 4-5
Ephesians 2
Ezekiel 35
Psalm 85

"Our faith as to the present is revived by glad memories of the past."

Charles H. Spurgeon
(1834-1892)

OCTOBER 3

READINGS

1 Kings 6
Ephesians 3
Ezekiel 36
Psalm 86

"This day I set apart as a day of fasting and prayer in reference, particularly, to my dear little Joshua; that, having been graciously carried through his weaning, he may be wholly the Lord's." *(A mother's concern over her child)*

Susan Huntington
(1791-1823)

OCTOBER 4

READINGS

1 Kings 7
Ephesians 4
Ezekiel 37
Psalms 87-88

"The Lord condescends to invite Himself to come under the filthy roofs of the houses of your souls. Do not be afraid of entertaining Him; He will fill you with all peace and joy in believing."

George Whitefield
(1714-1770)

OCTOBER 5

READINGS

1 Kings 8
Ephesians 5
Ezekiel 38
Psalm 89

"Anything that cools my love for Christ is the world."

John Wesley
(1703-1791)

OCTOBER 6

READINGS

1 Kings 9
Ephesians 6
Ezekiel 39
Psalm 90

"If you die wrong the first time, you cannot come back to die better a second time. If you die without Christ, you cannot come back to be converted and die a believer - you have but once to die. Pray that you may find Christ before death finds you."

Robert M. McCheyne
(1813-1843)

OCTOBER 7

READINGS

1 Kings 10
Philippians 1
Ezekiel 40
Psalm 91

"We must walk very close to a companion if we would have his shadow fall on us." *(concerning abiding under the shadow of the Almighty)*

**Mary Duncan
(1825-1865)**

OCTOBER 8

READINGS

1 Kings 11
Philippians 2
Ezekiel 41
Psalms 92-93

"Some people stumble over their intellect and say they can't understand religion. Many parts of the Bible I don't understand, but I am not going to fight against my Lord with my puny reason."

**Dwight L. Moody
(1837-1899)**

OCTOBER 9

READINGS

1 Kings 12
Philippians 3
Ezekiel 42
Psalm 94

"There is nothing like faith to help at a pinch; faith dissolves doubts as the sun dries away the mists."

**John Bunyan
(1628-1688)**

OCTOBER 10

READINGS

1 Kings 13
Philippians 4
Ezekiel 43
Psalms 95-96

"The great mark of a person who is waiting for the Lord is that he is looking round to see that others are ready for Him."

J. B. Stoney
(1815-1897)

OCTOBER 11

READINGS

1 Kings 14
Colossians 1
Ezekiel 44
Psalms 97-98

"Better to have a dog that will, by his barking, tell us a thief is in our yard, than one that will sit still and let us be robbed before we have any notice of our danger." *(concerning a troubled conscience)*

William Gurnall
(1617-1679)

OCTOBER 12

READINGS

1 Kings 15
Colossians 2
Ezekiel 45
Psalms 99-101

"Let fire, the cross, the letting out of beasts upon me, breaking of my bones, the tearing of my members, the grinding of my whole body, and the torments of the devils come upon me; so be it, (that) I may get Christ."

Jeremiah Burroughs
(1599-1646)

OCTOBER 13

READINGS

1 Kings 16
Colossians 3
Ezekiel 46
Psalm 102

"Sincerity is the holy oil which makes the wheels of the soul run nimbly, even in the difficult paths of obedience."

John Flavel
(1627-1691)

OCTOBER 14

READINGS

1 Kings 17
Colossians 4
Ezekiel 47
Psalm 103

"Despise not a man being a sinner, for though he be evil today, he may turn tomorrow."

William Perkins
(1558-1602)

OCTOBER 15

READINGS

1 Kings 18
1 Thessalonians 1
Ezekiel 48
Psalm 104

"The pure water should be allowed to flow from the heart of God to the heart of the sinner, without receiving a tinge from the channel through which it flows." *(written to an evangelist concerning preaching)*

Charles H. Mackintosh
(1820-1896)

OCTOBER 16

READINGS

1 Kings 19
1 Thessalonians 2
Daniel 1
Psalm 105

"The Word written is not only a rule of knowledge, but a rule of obedience; it is not only to mend our sight, but to mend our pace. Reading without practice will be but a torch to light men to hell."

**Thomas Watson
(1620-1686)**

OCTOBER 17

READINGS

1 Kings 20
1 Thessalonians 3
Daniel 2
Psalm 106

"You will never know how easy the yoke of Christ is till it is bound about your neck, nor how light His burden is till you have taken it up."

**Thomas Cole
(1627-1697)**

OCTOBER 18

READINGS

1 Kings 21
1 Thessalonians 4
Daniel 3
Psalm 107

"This keeps some of you from secret prayer, from worshipping God in your family, from going to lay your case before ministers, from openly confessing Christ. You that have felt God's love and Spirit, **dash this idol to pieces!**" *(concerning the fear of man)*

**Robert M. McCheyne
(1813-1843)**

99

OCTOBER 19

READINGS

1 Kings 22
1 Thessalonians 5
Daniel 4
Psalms 108-109

"Men can do little with their arm, but God can do all things with a glance."

Charles H. Spurgeon
(1834-1892)

OCTOBER 20

READINGS

2 Kings 1
2 Thessalonians 1
Daniel 5
Psalms 110-111

"Let us remember, that whilst we are in this world, we sojourn in a strange land, and are at a distance from our home; and, therefore, do not let us be inordinately affected with anything in it."

Philip Doddridge
(1702-1751)

OCTOBER 21

READINGS

2 Kings 2
2 Thessalonians 2
Daniel 6
Psalms 112-113

"Fire trieth iron, and temptation a just man. Temptation shows us what we are."

Thomas a Kempis
(1380-1471)

OCTOBER 22

READINGS

2 Kings 3
2 Thessalonians 3
Daniel 7
Psalms 114-115

"All your carnal reasonings and logical subtleties can never overthrow the plain Word of God."

John Fletcher
(1729-1785)

OCTOBER 23

READINGS

2 Kings 4
1 Timothy 1
Daniel 8
Psalm 116

"I would rather have a moderately small meeting of earnest Christians than to have it packed with thousands of careless people." *(concerning Christian training)*

Dwight L. Moody
(1837-1899)

OCTOBER 24

READINGS

2 Kings 5
1 Timothy 2
Daniel 9
Psalms 117-118

"He needs never be idle that hath so much business to do with his own soul."

George Swinnock
(1627-1673)

OCTOBER 25

READINGS

2 Kings 6
1 Timothy 3
Daniel 10
Psalm 119:1-24

"Take God into thy counsel. Heaven overlooks hell. God at any time can tell thee what plots are hatching there against thee."

William Gurnall
(1617-1679)

OCTOBER 26

READINGS

2 Kings 7
1 Timothy 4
Daniel 11
Psalm 119:25-48

"Remember that 'difficulty' is a word which has no meaning when applied to Him: it is not in Heaven's vocabulary; power belongs to God. Look out of yourself and altogether upon Him."

John Summerfield
(1770-1825)

OCTOBER 27

READINGS

2 Kings 8
1 Timothy 5
Daniel 12
Psalm 119:49-72

"Oh let every trial teach me more of Thy peace in my conscience, and more of Thy love in my heart, that I may keep on in a steady course, walking humbly with my God."

William Romaine
(1714-1795)

OCTOBER 28

READINGS

**2 Kings 9
1 Timothy 6
Hosea 1
Psalm 119:73-96**

"Babes *(spiritually newborn and unlearned)* are as capable of knowing the things of God as the wise and prudent; and they are often hid from these when they are revealed to those."

**Jonathon Edwards
(1703-1758)**

OCTOBER 29

READINGS

**2 Kings 10-11
2 Timothy 1
Hosea 2
Psalm 119:97-120**

"I wish to live in a reasonable independence of this world; to take what my God gives me thankfully, and wish for nothing more."

**Susan Huntington
(1791-1823)**

OCTOBER 30

READINGS

**2 Kings 12
2 Timothy 2
Hosea 3-4
Psalm 119:121-144**

"The most of God's people are contented to be saved from the hell that is **without**. They are not so anxious to be saved from the hell that is within."

**Robert M. McCheyne
(1813-1843)**

OCTOBER
31

"Our only refuge, our only resource, our only strength, our only comfort, our only authority, is the precious Word of God. Take away that, and we have absolutely nothing; give us that, and we want no more."

Charles H. Mackintosh
(1820-1896)

PAUL TAKEN BY THE CHIEF CAPTAIN

NOVEMBER
1

"He is the most thankful man that treasures up the mercies of God in his memory, and can feed his faith with what God hath done for him, so as to walk in the strength thereof in present straits."

William Gurnall
(1617-1679)

NOVEMBER 2

READINGS

**2 Kings 15
Titus 1
Hosea 8
Psalms 123-125**

"God will neither expect nor desire his blessing without exertion; for it has always been God's way to crown only those that run the race that is set before them, and fight the good fight of faith."

**William Jay
(1769-1853)**

NOVEMBER 3

READINGS

**2 Kings 16
Titus 2
Hosea 9
Psalms 126-128**

"If the veil of the world's machinery were lifted off, how much we would find is done in answer to the prayers of God's children."

**Robert M. McCheyne
(1813-1843)**

NOVEMBER 4

READINGS

**2 Kings 17
Titus 3
Hosea 10
Psalms 129-131**

"He that loves a tree, hates the worm that consumes it; he that loves a garment, hates the moth that eats it; he that loveth life, abhorreth death; and he that loves the Lord hates **everything** that offends Him."

**William Couper
(1566-1619)**

NOVEMBER 5

READINGS

2 Kings 18
Philemon 1
Hosea 11
Psalms 132-134

"Let no cross be considered too heavy to be borne in following Christ; no loss too great to be sustained for Christ; and no path too holy in going after Christ."

James B. Taylor
(1801-1829)

NOVEMBER 6

READINGS

2 Kings 19
Hebrews 1
Hosea 12
Psalms 135-136

"Death brings no peril to a child of God; and ought to be no more an object of his fear than the approach of sleep at the close of day."

John M. Mason
(1770-1829)

NOVEMBER 7

READINGS

2 Kings 20
Hebrews 2
Hosea 13
Psalms 137-138

"The Christian that is truly acquainted with Him, enamored with the brightness of His beauty, can generously trample upon the smilings of the world with one foot, and upon her frownings with the other."

Robert Leighton
(1613-1684)

NOVEMBER 8

READINGS

2 Kings 21
Hebrews 3
Hosea 14
Psalm 139

"He who makes little of God makes much of himself. They who forget adoration fall into adulation."

Charles H. Spurgeon
(1834-1892)

NOVEMBER 9

READINGS

2 Kings 22
Hebrews 4
Joel 1
Psalms 140-141

"I have so much to do that I cannot get on without three hours a day of praying."

Martin Luther
(1483-1546)

NOVEMBER 10

READINGS

2 Kings 23
Hebrews 5
Joel 2
Psalm 142

"A righteous man may make a righteous work, but no work of an unrighteous man can make him righteous. The tree makes the fruit, not the fruit the tree; and therefore the tree must be good before the fruit can be good."

Thomas Boston
(1676-1732)

NOVEMBER 11

READINGS

2 Kings 24
Hebrews 6
Joel 3
Psalm 143

"If God were not my friend, Satan would not be so much my enemy."

Thomas Brooks
(1608-1680)

NOVEMBER 12

READINGS

2 Kings 25
Hebrews 7
Amos 1
Psalm 144

"God fails not to sow blessings in the furrows, which the plowers plow upon the back of the church." *(concerning persecution)*

Jeremy Taylor
(1613-1667)

NOVEMBER 13

READINGS

1 Chronicles 1-2
Hebrews 8
Amos 2
Psalm 145

"I would rather know how to pray like Daniel than to preach like Gabriel."

Dwight L. Moody
(1837-1899)

NOVEMBER 14

READINGS

1 Chronicles 3-4
Hebrews 9
Amos 3
Psalms 146-147

"Scripture is the Word of God, and it judges man thoroughly. It lays bare the very roots of his nature - it opens up the foundations of his moral being."

Charles H. Mackintosh
(1820-1896)

NOVEMBER 15

READINGS

1 Chronicles 5-6
Hebrews 10
Amos 4
Psalms 148-150

"Many follow Jesus unto the breaking of bread; but few to the drinking of the cup of His passion."

Thomas a Kempis
(1380-1471)

NOVEMBER 16

READINGS

1 Chronicles 7-8
Hebrews 11
Amos 5
Luke 1:1-38

"I consider myself as a stone in the hands of a carver, whereof He wills to make a statue; presenting myself thus before God, I beseech Him to render me entirely like Himself, and to fashion in my soul His Perfect Image."

Nicolas Herman
(Brother Lawrence)
(1611-1691)

NOVEMBER 17

READINGS

1 Chronicles 9-10
Hebrews 12
Amos 6
Luke 1:39-80

"Resignation to the will of God frees the mind from a grievous bondage, the bondage of earthly pursuits and expectations. Whatever God wills is pleasing to the resigned soul."

**Robert Walker
(1716-1783)**

NOVEMBER 18

READINGS

1 Chronicles 11-12
Hebrews 13
Amos 7
Luke 2

"There is a living God. He has spoken His Word. He means just what He says, and will do all that He has promised."

**James Hudson Taylor
(1832-1905)**

NOVEMBER 19

READINGS

1 Chronicles 13-14
James 1
Amos 8
Luke 3

"Trials make the promise sweet,
Trials give new life to prayer;
Trials bring me to His feet,
Lay me low, and keep me there."

**Robert M. McCheyne
(1813-1843)**

NOVEMBER 20

READINGS

1 Chronicles 15
James 2
Amos 9
Luke 4

"Set a strong guard about thy outward senses: these are Satan's landing places, especially the eye and the ear."

William Gurnall
(1617-1679)

NOVEMBER 21

READINGS

1 Chronicles 16
James 3
Obadiah 1
Luke 5

"If the queen be pleased to release me, I will thank her; if she will imprison me, I will thank her; if she will burn me, I will thank her." *(martyr - burned at stake)*

John Bradford
(1510-1555)

NOVEMBER 22

READINGS

1 Chronicles 17
James 4
Jonah 1
Luke 6

"There was a day when I died, utterly died to my opinions, preferences, tastes, and will - died to the world, its approval or censure - died to the approval or blame even of my brethren and friends, and since then I have studied only to show myself approved unto God."

George Mueller
(1856-1898)

NOVEMBER 23

READINGS

1 Chronicles 18
James 5
Jonah 2
Luke 7

"For men to abuse things on earth, and live to themselves, is the same rebellion against God as for angels to abuse things in heaven."

**William Law
(1686-1761)**

NOVEMBER 24

READINGS

1 Chronicles 19-20
1 Peter 1
Jonah 3
Luke 8

"Man's extremity is God's opportunity. Jesus will come to deliver just when His needy ones shall sigh, as if all hope had gone forever."

**Charles H. Spurgeon
(1834-1892)**

NOVEMBER 25

READINGS

1 Chronicles 21
1 Peter 2
Jonah 4
Luke 9

"The grand business of the servant of Christ is to obey. His object should not be to do a great deal, but simply to do what he is told."

**Charles H. Mackintosh
(1820-1896)**

NOVEMBER 26

READINGS

1 Chronicles 22
1 Peter 3
Micah 1
Luke 10

"Speak every time, my dear brother, as if it were your last; weep out, if possible, every argument; and compel them to cry, 'Behold, how He loves us'."

George Whitefield
(1714-1770)

NOVEMBER 27

READINGS

1 Chronicles 23
1 Peter 4
Micah 2
Luke 11

"When I really enjoy God I feel my desires of Him the more insatiable and my thirstings after holiness the more unquenchable. O' this pleasing pain. It makes my soul press after God."

David Brainerd
(1717-1747)

NOVEMBER 28

READINGS

1 Chronicles 24-25
1 Peter 5
Micah 3
Luke 12

"I long for love without any coldness, light without dimness, and purity without spot or wrinkle."

Robert M. McCheyne
(1813-1843)

NOVEMBER 29

"If we teach our children as we ought to do, instead of Sunday being the dreariest, dullest, tiresomest day of the week to them, it will be the brightest, happiest day of the whole seven."

**Dwight L. Moody
(1837-1899)**

NOVEMBER 30

"In our way to heaven, we need not only a rule and path, but a guide. The rule is the Law of God; but the guide is the Spirit of God."

**Thomas Manton
(1620-1677**

JESUS AND THE WOMAN TAKEN IN ADULTERY

DECEMBER 1

READINGS

1 Chronicles 29
2 Peter 3
Micah 6
Luke 15

"Our tiny springs would soon dry up if not kept in unbroken connection with the everflowing Fountain."

**Charles H. Mackintosh
(1820-1896)**

DECEMBER 2

READINGS

2 Chronicles 1
1 John 1
Micah 7
Luke 16

"As we try God's Word, so God's Word tries us; and happy (are we) if, when we are tried, we come forth as gold."

**William Jay
(1769-1853)**

DECEMBER 3

READINGS

2 Chronicles 2
1 John 2
Nahum 1
Luke 17

"God's time must be our time, or it will come to pass that, when time closes, we shall look in vain for space for repentance."

**Charles H. Spurgeon
(1834-1892)**

DECEMBER 4

READINGS

2 Chronicles 3-4
1 John 3
Nahum 2
Luke 18

"Remember Jesus **for** us is all our righteousness before a holy God, and Jesus **in** us is all our strength in an ungodly world."

**Robert M. McCheyne
(1813-1843)**

DECEMBER 5

READINGS

2 Chronicles 5-6:11
1 John 4
Nahum 3
Luke 19

"Better it is for thee to have little, than much of that which may make thee proud."

**Thomas a Kempis
(1380-1471)**

DECEMBER 6

READINGS

2 Chr. 6:12-42
1 John 5
Habakkuk 1
Luke 20

"Prayer is the leech of the soul, that sucks out the venom and swelling thereof."

**Martin Luther
(1483-1546)**

DECEMBER 7

READINGS

2 Chronicles 7
2 John 1
Habakkuk 2
Luke 21

"If I ever get to Heaven, it will be because God pleases and nothing else; for I never did anything of myself but get away from God." *(from his private journal)*

David Brainerd
(1717-1747)

DECEMBER 8

READINGS

2 Chronicles 8
3 John 1
Habakkuk 3
Luke 22

"The Spirit of Love waits to fill us as soon as we are ready to buy without holding back part of the price. You must give up all - all you have and all you are."

William Law
(1686-1761)

DECEMBER 9

READINGS

2 Chronicles 9
Jude 1
Zephaniah 1
Luke 23

"We are so inclined to sin that we need strong restraints, and so swelled with a natural pride against God that we need thorns in the flesh to **let out** the corrupt matter."

Stephen Charnock
(1628-1680)

DECEMBER 10

READINGS

2 Chronicles 10
Revelation 1
Zephaniah 2
Luke 24

"When the corn is near ripe, it bows the head and stoops lower than when it was green. When the people of God are near ripe for Heaven, they grow more humble and self-denying than in the days of their first profession."

**John Flavel
(1627-1691)**

DECEMBER 11

READINGS

2 Chronicles 11-12
Revelation 2
Zephaniah 3
John 1

"Precious things are usually hidden."

**Joseph Caryl
(1602-1673)**

DECEMBER 12

READINGS

2 Chronicles 13
Revelation 3
Haggai 1
John 2

"There is reason to think that there are many in this congregation now hearing this discourse that will actually be the subjects of this very miscry to all eternity. How many is it likely will remember this discourse in **hell**!" *(sermon: Sinners in the Hands of an Angry God)*

**Jonathon Edwards
(1703-1758)**

DECEMBER 13

READINGS

2 Chronicles 14-15
Revelation 4
Haggai 2
John 3

"The motion of our **praise** must be like the motion of our pulse, which beats as long as life lasts."

**Thomas Watson
(1620-1686)**

DECEMBER 14

READINGS

2 Chronicles 16
Revelation 5
Zechariah 1
John 4

"Men may die like lambs and yet have their place forever with the goats."

**Matthew Henry
(1662-1714)**

DECEMBER 15

READINGS

2 Chronicles 17
Revelation 6
Zechariah 2
John 5

"A man who wants to work for God can find work, and nobody can stop him."

**Dwight L. Moody
(1837-1899)**

DECEMBER 16

READINGS

2 Chronicles 18
Revelation 7
Zechariah 3
John 6

"Love at first sight is no uncommon thing when Jesus is the wooer. His Gospel is, in some cases, no sooner heard than believed."

**Charles H. Spurgeon
(1834-1892)**

DECEMBER 17

READINGS

2 Chronicles 19-20
Revelation 8
Zechariah 4
John 7

"The Lord would rather have your company than your property."

**J. B. Stoney
(1815-1897)**

DECEMBER 18

READINGS

2 Chronicles 21
Revelation 9
Zechariah 5
John 8

"Value yourself by your inheritance in the other world, and not by your honour and riches in this."

**William Gurnall
(1617-1679)**

DECEMBER 19

READINGS

2 Chronicles 22-23
Revelation 10
Zechariah 6
John 9

"Nothing that the world contains is worth the life and consecration of an immortal soul."

Henry Drummond
(1851-1897)

DECEMBER 20

READINGS

2 Chronicles 24
Revelation 11
Zechariah 7
John 10

"Where there is no fervency on our part, no wonder if there is no answer on God's."

Robert South
(1633-1716)

DECEMBER 21

READINGS

2 Chronicles 25
Revelation 12
Zechariah 8
John 11

"It is notable that our Lord Jesus, when there were but five barley loaves and two fishes, lifted up His eyes and gave thanks."

Thomas Manton
(1620-1677)

DECEMBER 22

READINGS

2 Chronicles 26
Revelation 13
Zechariah 9
John 12

"Though there was much smoke, yet every day I had more and more convincing proof that a blessed Gospel fire had been kindled in the hearts both of ministers and people." *(concerning evangelistic work in America)*

**George Whitefield
(1714-1770)**

DECEMBER 23

READINGS

2 Chronicles 27-28
Revelation 14
Zechariah 10
John 13

"Because Christ was forsaken for a time, you shall not be forsaken forever, for He was forsaken for you."

**John Flavel
(1627-1691)**

DECEMBER 24

READINGS

2 Chronicles 29
Revelation 15
Zechariah 11
John 14

"Use a few spare half-hours in seeking after the lambs on the week days. This will prove to the parents that you are in earnest. To bring one child to the bosom of Christ would be reward for all our pains in eternity." *(to Sunday School teachers)*

**Robert M. McCheyne
(1813-1843)**

DECEMBER 25

READINGS

2 Chronicles 30
Revelation 16
Zechariah 12-13:1
John 15

"On great occasions kings put on their finest apparel, but God wrapped himself in dust when He entered the world."

Stephen Jeffreys
(1876-1943)

DECEMBER 26

READINGS

2 Chronicles 31
Revelation 17
Zechariah 13:2-9
John 16

"Hold yourself in prayer before God, like a poor, dumb, paralytic beggar at a rich man's gate."

Nicolas Herman
(Brother Lawrence)
(1611-1691)

DECEMBER 27

READINGS

2 Chronicles 32
Revelation 18
Zechariah 14
John 17

"Adversity is the diamond dust Heaven polishes its jewels with."

Robert Leighton
(1611-1684)

DECEMBER 28

READINGS

2 Chronicles 33
Revelation 19
Malachi 1
John 18

"We should ever remember that those whom God uses much in public He trains in secret; and further, that all His most honored servants have been more occupied with their Master than with their work."

Charles H. Mackintosh
(1820-1896)

DECEMBER 29

READINGS

2 Chronicles 34
Revelation 20
Malachi 2
John 19

"As every good master or father of a family is a good preacher to his own family; so every good Christian is a good preacher to his own soul."

Richard Baxter
(1615-1691)

DECEMBER 30

READINGS

2 Chronicles 35
Revelation 21
Malachi 3
John 20

"Your children have souls, and these God sets you to watch over. It will be a poor account at the last day, if you can only say, 'Lord, here are my children, I bred them complete gentlemen (and) left them rich and wealthy'."

William Gurnall
(1617-1679)

READINGS

2 Chronicles 36
Revelation 22
Malachi 4
John 21

"Life itself is vanishing fast.　Make haste for eternity."

Robert M. McCheyne
(1813-1843)

THE DELIVERANCE OF PETER FROM PRISON

For additional copies of
On Earth as it is in Heaven
please contact:

Destiny Image
P.O. Box 310
Shippensburg, PA 17257
or call toll free
1-800-722-6774

PRAYER REQUESTS

PRAYER REQUESTS

PRAYER REQUESTS

PRAYER REQUESTS